Copyright© Disclai

*This material is for your own use only. If you're thinking abou
please keep in mind the trust we've built thus far, and re*

GW01454934

Publisher:

Good Company OÜ – drills.golf
Sepapaja 6, 15551 Tallinn, Estonia

www.drills.golf

support@drills.golf

Meet Your Drills

...as if you were looking at all of them **from the hilltop**...

Putting Drills **24 Drills in eBook**

Use These Drills During 🏆

Competition and Non-Competition Season

Expert Title of eBook

All-Round Matrix

Skills You Will Learn 📈

✅ Develop Consistent Stroke

✅ Learn How to Score

✅ Create Better Alignment

Purpose of Drills 😇

All encompassing collection of putting drills - develop technique, learn how to score, and learn mental imagery. If you're stuck repeating the same drills, use this combination of drills to break the monotony.

Vision 🤨 of eBook

All-Rounded **combination of 24 drills and challenges**. This Matrix utilizes both **Static exercises** with conventional stationary execution and **Dynamic exercises** with plenty of movement around the hole.

Additionally, it is a mix of performance drills utilizing challenges and goal-oriented exercises, and technical drills utilizing high number of repetitions from a single stand. All-Round Matrix is a good choice for both competitive and non-competitive season.

Tips: How to Read The Drills

Get the most out of each drill. Each drill has the following information to inform your practice sessions and help you find the perfect drill for your next practice session.

Short	**Mid**	Long

Putt from different distances.

- **Short** [3,6,9 ft | 1,2,3 m]
- **Mid** [10-20 ft | 4-7 m]
- **Long** [25-50 ft | 8-15 m]

Off-Season Activity

Practice **In-Season drills** to prepare for your next tournament.
Practice **Off-Season drills** to work on technique and relax.
Practice **Pre-Season drills** to combine technique and performance.

Number of Players. Easily find the drill you can play with your friends.
Coaching? Quickly find the drill that facilitates the needs of your team practice.

E M H

Some drills are easier, some harder. Use difficulty buttons to find the drill with the right difficulty level for your needs.

- **Easy** [Green Button]
- **Medium** [Orange Button]
- **Hard** [Red Button]

Designed for	
• Club Control	• Aim/Alignment
• Ball Control	• Precision/Accuracy
• Challenge	• Distance Control
	• Visualization/Read
	• Scoring
Primary Skills	*Secondary Skills*

Know what skills you are learning every time you step on the putting green.

Give yourself direction with **Primary high-level Skills**, and Lean into **Secondary Skills** to learn specific golf skills.

---

15 – 20 min

Come prepared. Know exactly how much time you need to complete the drill. On average, the drills are designed for **40-80 repetitions**, or 15-20 minutes.

Short | Mid | Long

○ ○ **H**

15 – 20 min

Designed for

- Shot Shaping
- Performance

- Precision/Accuracy
- Distance Control
- Visualization/Read
- Scoring

Primary Skills | *Secondary Skills*

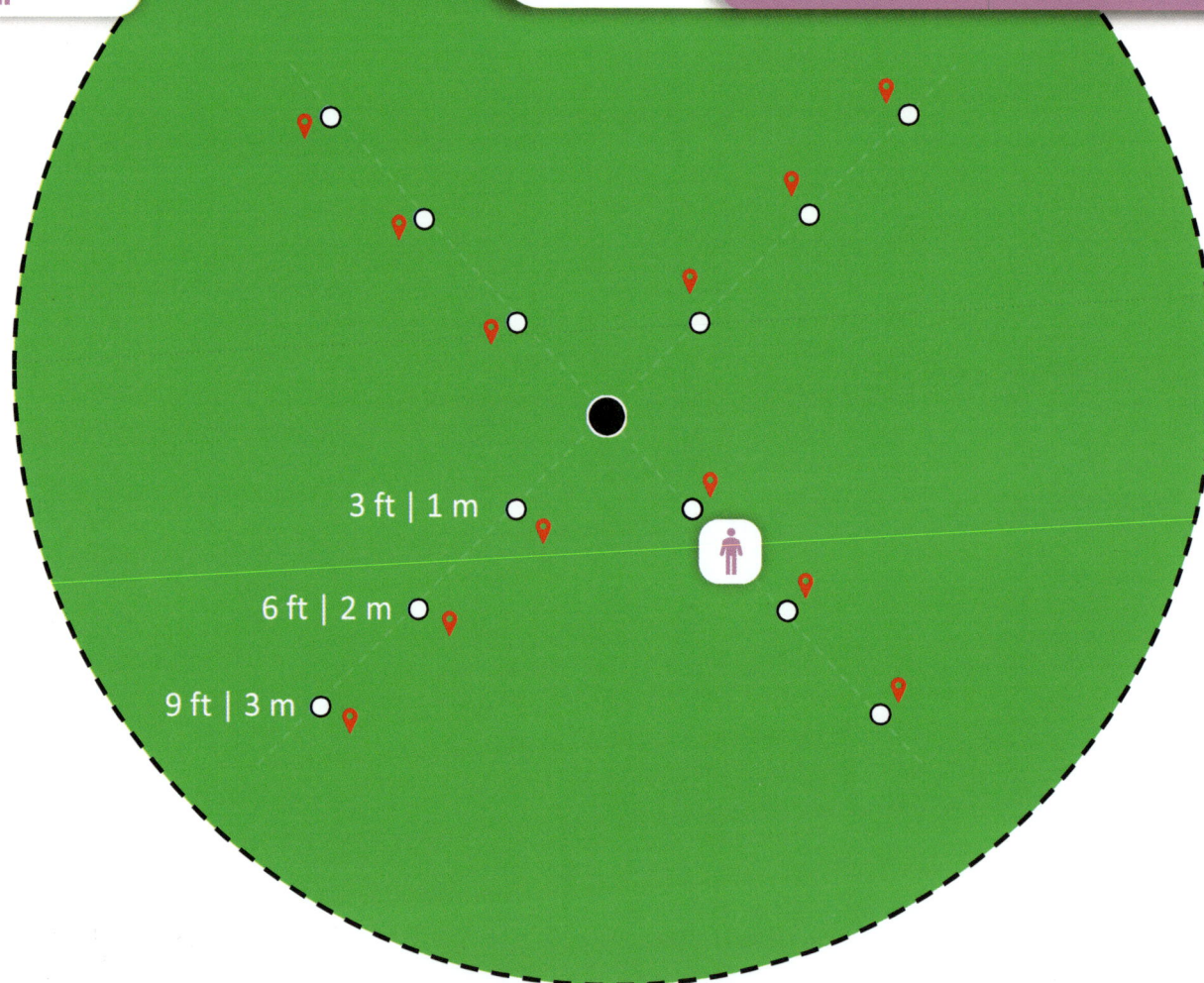

3 ft | 1 m

6 ft | 2 m

9 ft | 3 m

1010

Around the Hole: X Drill, in a Row

Complete one or both approaches.

✓ **Approach #1 (harder) – make 12 putts in a row.** Start at one side of the hole by making the shortest putt at **[3 ft | 1 m]**, then **[6 ft | 2 m]**, then **[9 ft | 3 m]**, and then on to the next line of putts. The goal is to make an entire X Drill in a row, all 12 putts. If any putt is missed, start over.

✓ **Approach #2 (easier) – make 3 putts in a row, 4 times.** Goal is to close all four sides of the hole, one side at a time. Hole 3 putts in a row **[3,6, and 9 ft | 1,2, and 3 m]** to close one side of the hole, then move on to the next side. Once one side is closed, do not go back to it. Each side is treated as a separate 3 in a row challenge. If any of the three putts are missed, start over with the first putt.

Setup* *position three tees at four sides of the hole (12 tees in total)*

M

15 – 20 min

Designed for

Primary Skills	Secondary Skills
• Shot Shaping	• Precision/Accuracy
• Performance	• Distance Control
	• Visualization/Read
	• Scoring

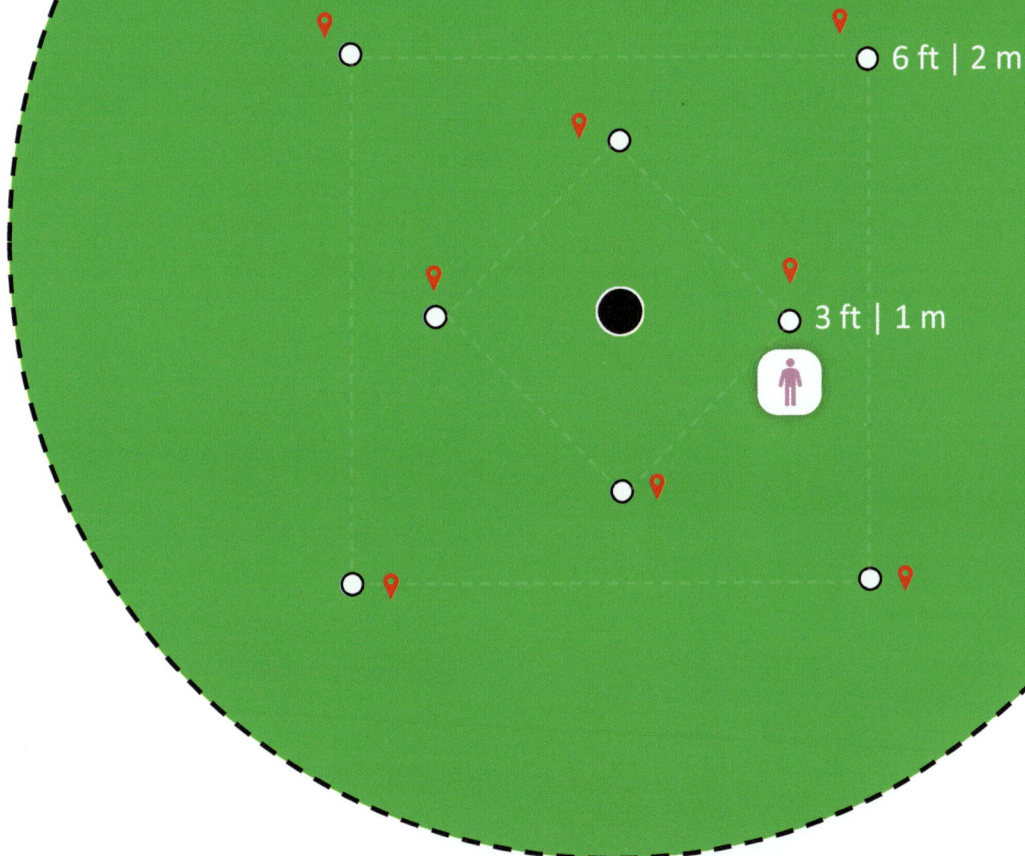

6 ft | 2 m

3 ft | 1 m

1011

Around the Hole: X1-X2, in a Row

Make 8 putts in a row to complete the challenge.

✓ Start from **[3 ft | 1m]** from one of the four sides of the hole. Once putt is holed, putt from the next closest tee in front **[6 ft | 2 m]**, then from the next closest **[3 ft | 1 m],** and so around. If any putt is missed, start over. Complete the challenge more than once.

Setup* *position four tees at an inside rectangle (shorter distance) and four tees at an outside rectangle (longer distance).*

M

15 – 20 min

Designed for

- Shot Shaping
- Performance
- Precision/Accuracy
- Distance Control
- Visualization/Read
- Scoring

Primary Skills *Secondary Skills*

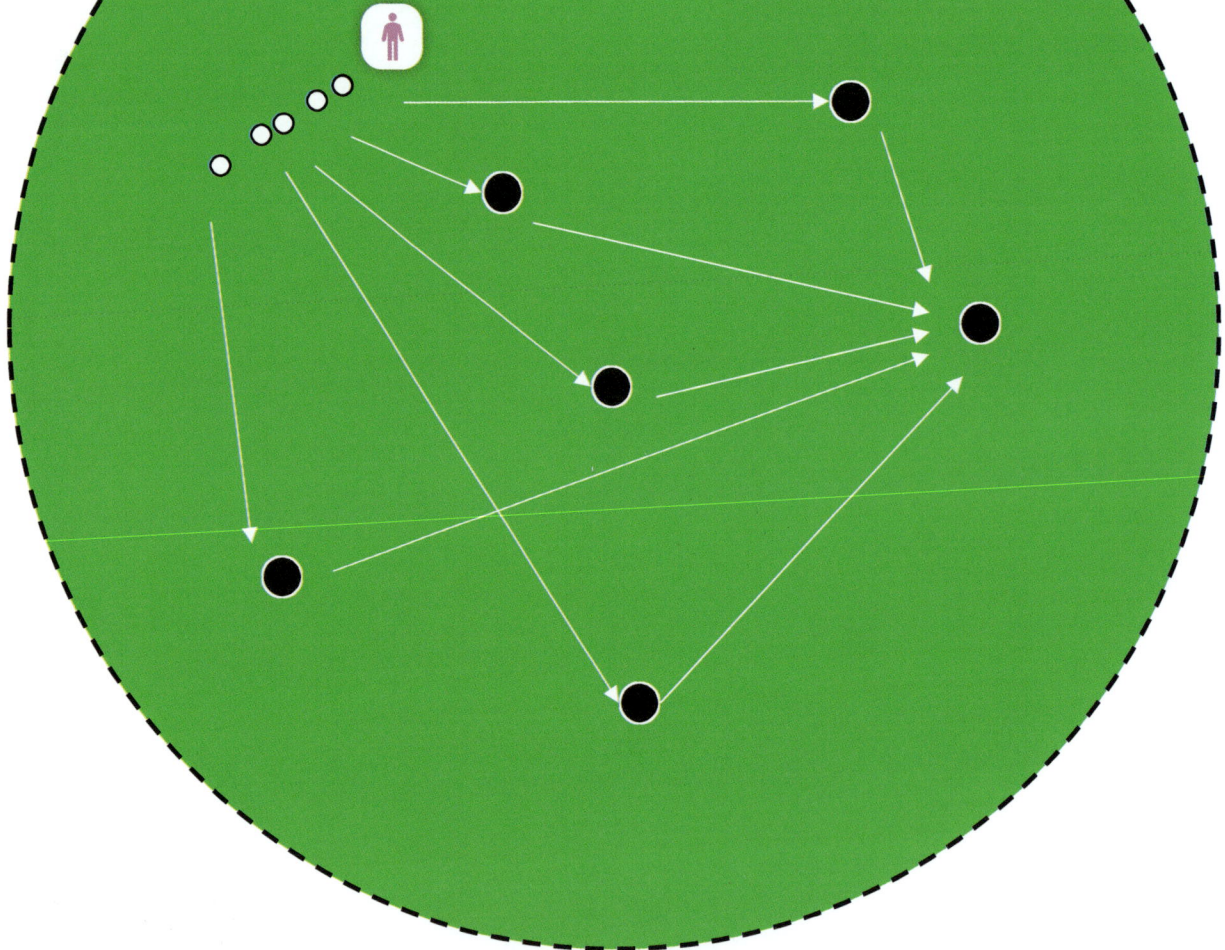

1012

Disperse, Gather – 5 Holes

Play stroke-play with 5 balls. Hit ~60 putts.

✓ Occupy a position on the green and hit 5 balls to 5 different holes (disperse). Finish the closest hole and immediately hit the next putt to an end (6th) hole (gather). Do the same for all other holes. Finish the hole and hit the ball to an end hole (gather). Then finish all the putts on the 6th hole. Once all the putts are made in the 6th hole, start again by dispersing the balls to 5 different holes. Count the total score relative to PAR (each hole is PAR 2). Go back and forth at least 3 times (~60 putts in total).

Designed for

- Shot Shaping
- Performance
- Distance Control
- Visualization/Read
- Scoring

15 – 20 min

Primary Skills   *Secondary Skills*

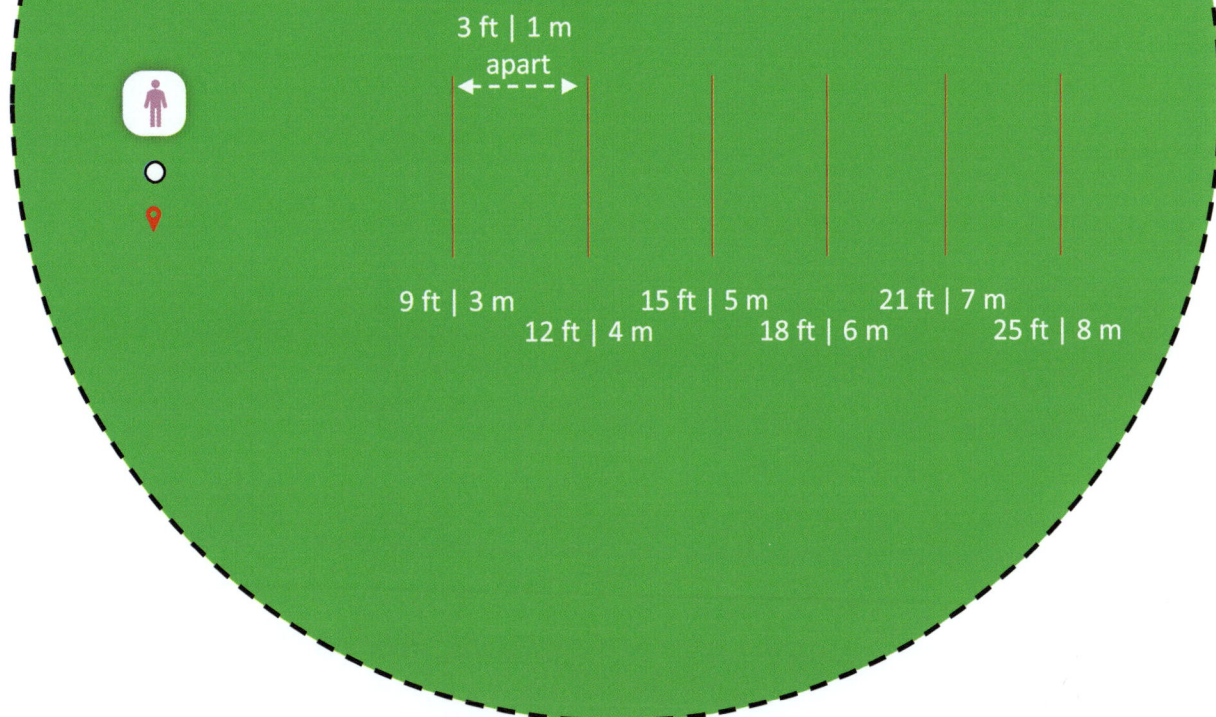

3 ft | 1 m apart

9 ft | 3 m
12 ft | 4 m
15 ft | 5 m
18 ft | 6 m
21 ft | 7 m
25 ft | 8 m

1015

Stop the Ball: Inside the Field, in a Row [Mid]

Stop 5 balls in a row – one inside each field – to complete the challenge. If miss, fall back two fields.

✓ **Approach #1 – short to long (easier).** The challenge is completed once five putts in a row are stopped inside five fields, each ball inside one field. Start with the first field, then advance to the next field. If any field is missed, fall back two fields.

✓ **Approach #2 – randomly (harder).** The challenge is completed once five putts in a row are stopped inside five fields, each ball inside one field, starting with any field and randomly choosing the next field. If any field is missed, start over from the beginning.

✓ Repeat the challenge more than once.

Setup * use 6 strings (or 12 tees) to make five fields *[3ft|1m apart]* at *[9,12,15,18,21,25 ft | 3,4,5,6,7,8 m]*

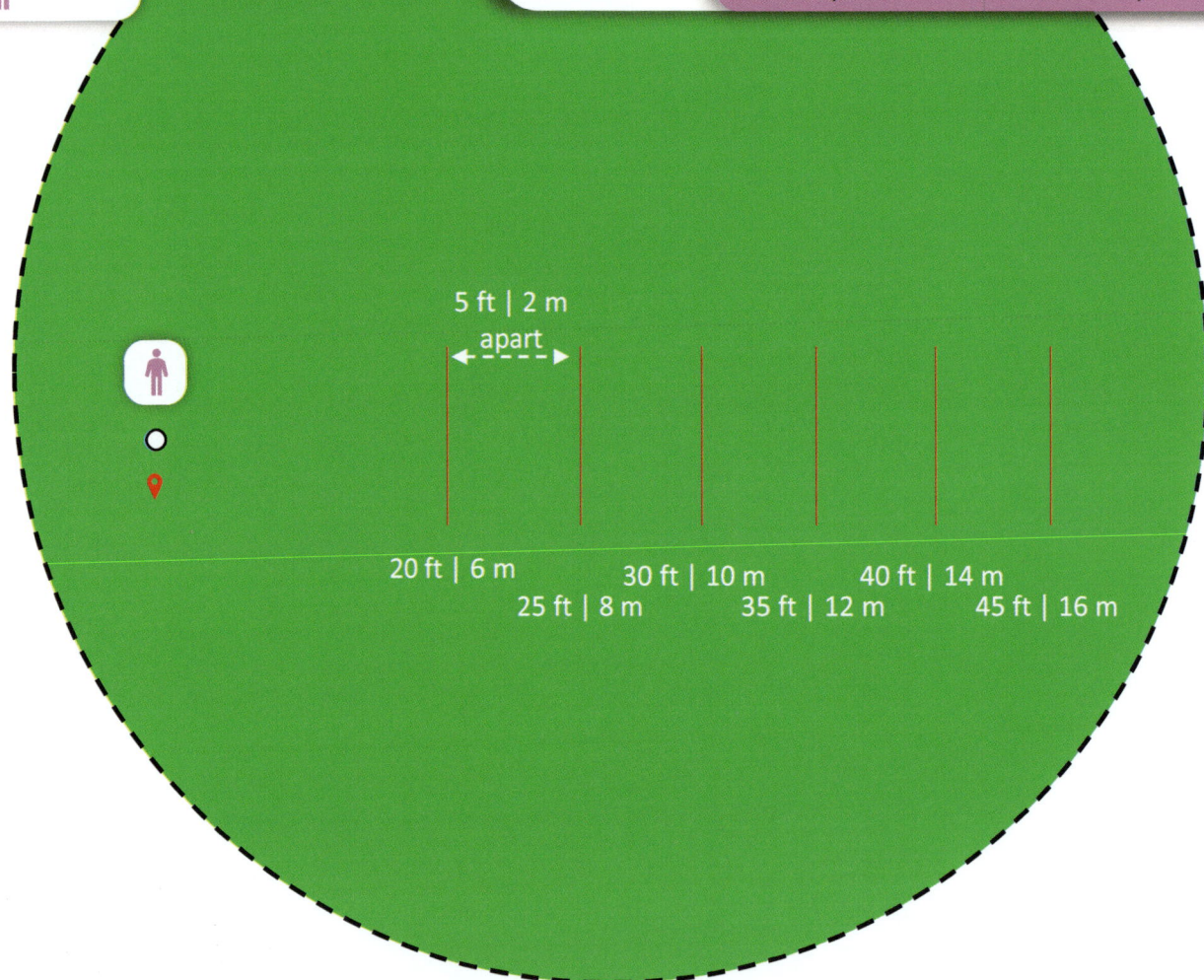

15 – 20 min

Designed for

- Shot Shaping
- Performance
- Distance Control
- Visualization/Read
- Scoring

Primary Skills | *Secondary Skills*

5 ft | 2 m
apart

20 ft | 6 m
25 ft | 8 m
30 ft | 10 m
35 ft | 12 m
40 ft | 14 m
45 ft | 16 m

1016

Stop the Ball: Inside the Field, in a Row [Long]

Stop 5 balls in a row – one inside each field – to complete the challenge. If miss, fall back two fields.

✓ **Approach #1 – short to long (easier).** The challenge is completed once five putts in a row are stopped inside five fields, each ball inside one field. Start with the first field, then advance to the next field. If any field is missed, fall back two fields.

✓ **Approach #2 – randomly (harder).** The challenge is completed once five putts in a row are stopped inside five fields, each ball inside one field, starting with any field and randomly choosing the next field. If any field is missed, start over from the beginning.

✓ Repeat the challenge more than once.

Setup* use 6 strings (or 12 tees) to make five fields [5 ft| 2 m apart] at [20,25,30,35,40,45 ft | 6,8,10,12,14,16 m]

M

15 – 20 min

Designed for

- Performance
- Distance Control
- Visualization/Read
- Scoring

Primary Skills | *Secondary Skills*

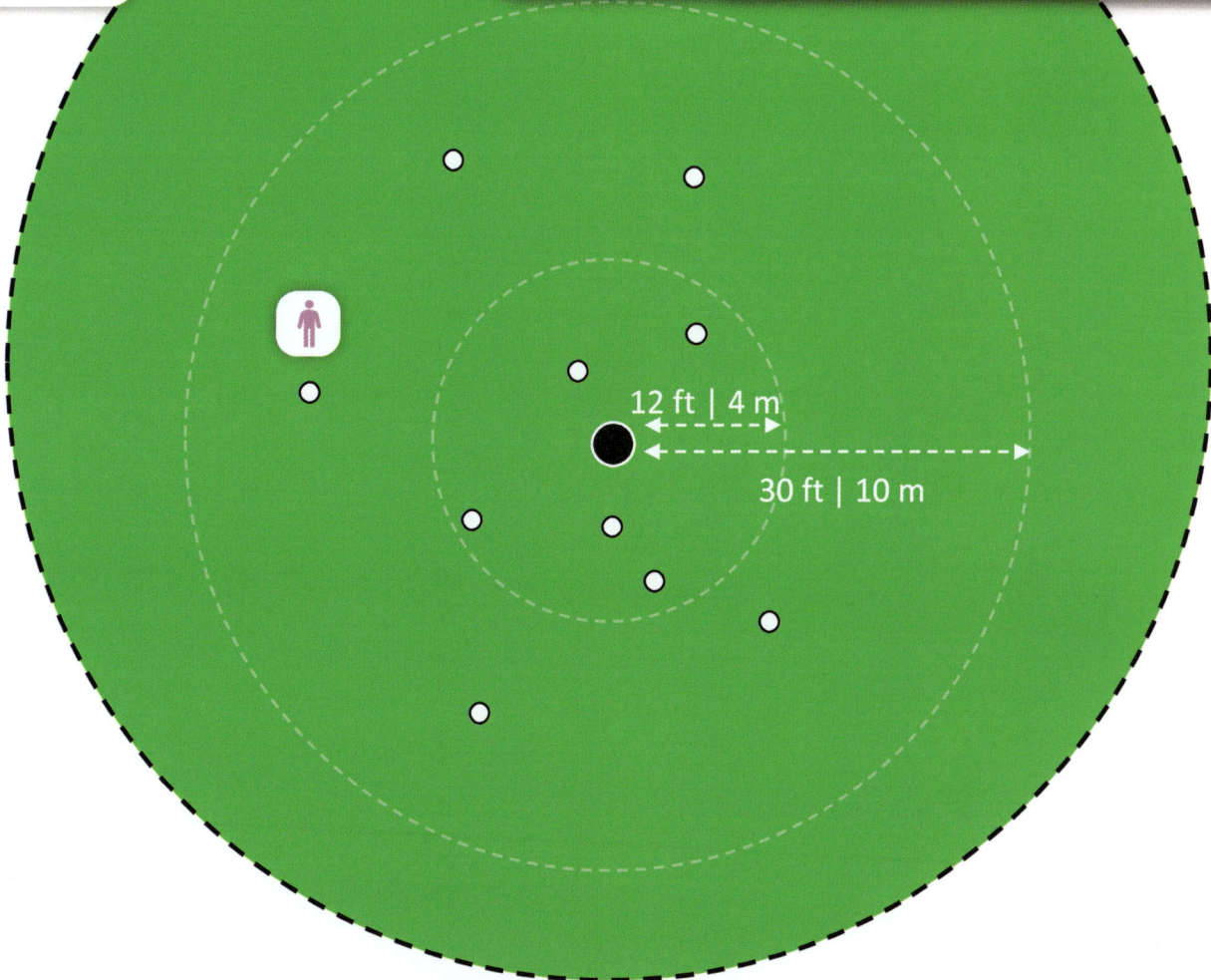

12 ft | 4 m

30 ft | 10 m

1022

Opportunities: 6-14 Greens in Regulation

Simulate real-life scenario with X number of birdie opportunities (Greens in Regulation).

✓ Start with **6 GIR** exercise; use 6 golf balls; randomly position half of the balls inside **[12 ft | 4 m]** radius and the other half between **[12 ft | 4 m]** and **[30 ft | 10 m]** radius. Finish all the putts and count the total score relative to PAR. Then complete the **8 GIR**; then **10 GIR**, **12 GIR** and **14 GIR**. Count the cumulative total score for all five GIR exercises (6, 8, 10, 12 and 14).

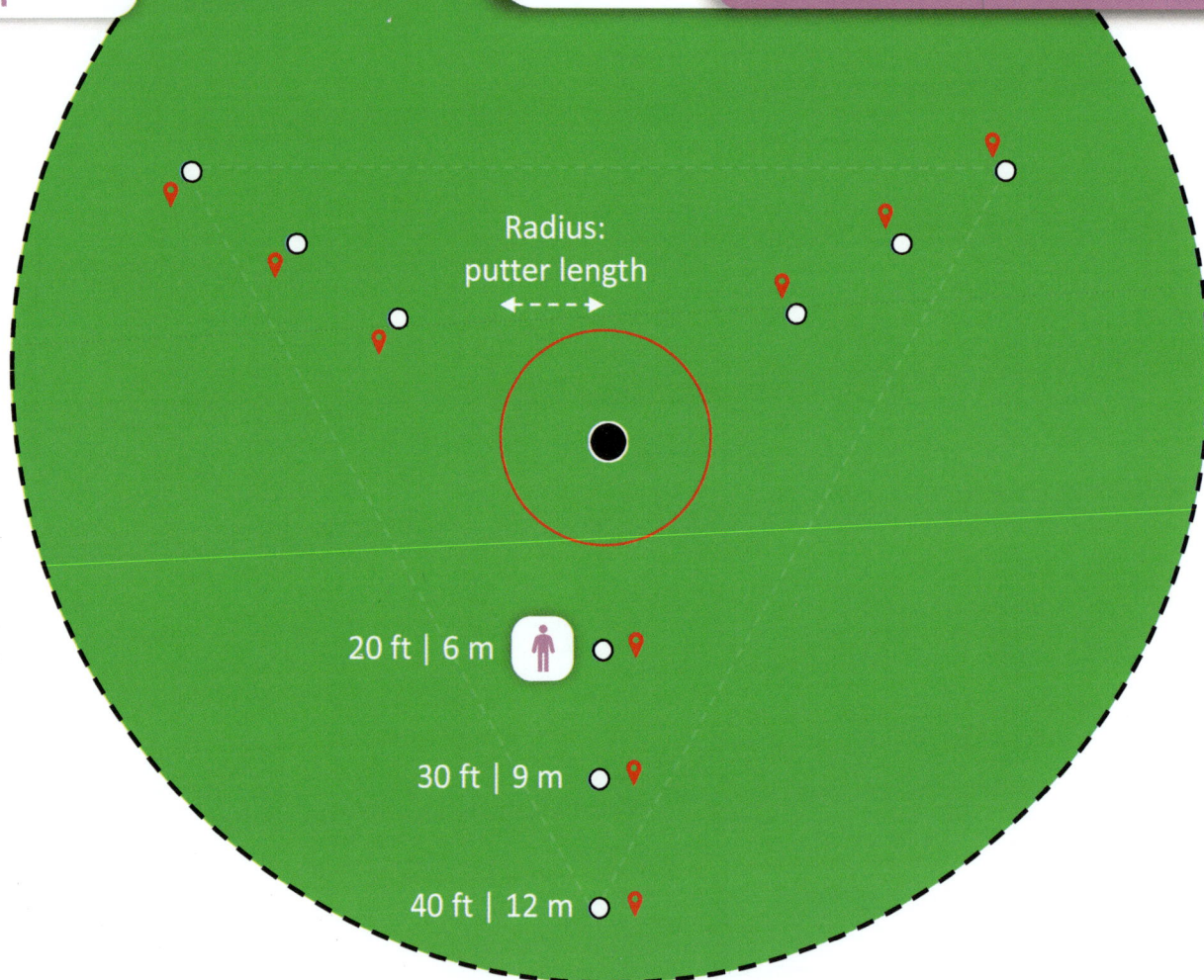

Designed for

- Shot Shaping
- Performance
- Precision/Accuracy
- Distance Control
- Visualization/Read
- Scoring

15 – 20 min

Primary Skills   *Secondary Skills*

Radius: putter length

20 ft | 6 m

30 ft | 9 m

40 ft | 12 m

1028

Stop the Ball: Circle, Three Tees Triangle, in a Row

Stop 9 balls in a row inside the circle to complete the challenge.

✓ Goal is to stop 9 balls in a row inside the circle. Start from one side of the hole from **[20 ft | 6 m]**, then advance to second **[30 ft | 9 m]** and third tee **[40 ft | 12 m]**. Then advance to the next **[20 ft | 6 m]** tee on the next side of the hole and progress until you stop all 9 balls in a row inside the circle. If at any time any ball misses the circle, start over from scratch. Complete the challenge more than once.

Setup position 9 tees, 3 tees on each side of the hole at **[20,30,40 ft | 6,9,12 m]**. *Use a string line to form a circle (radius is one putter length); or use several tees; or draw using chalk.*

H

15 – 20 min

Designed for

- Technique
- Shot Shaping
- Performance
- Aim/Alignment
- Distance Control
- Visualization/Read
- Scoring

Primary Skills | *Secondary Skills*

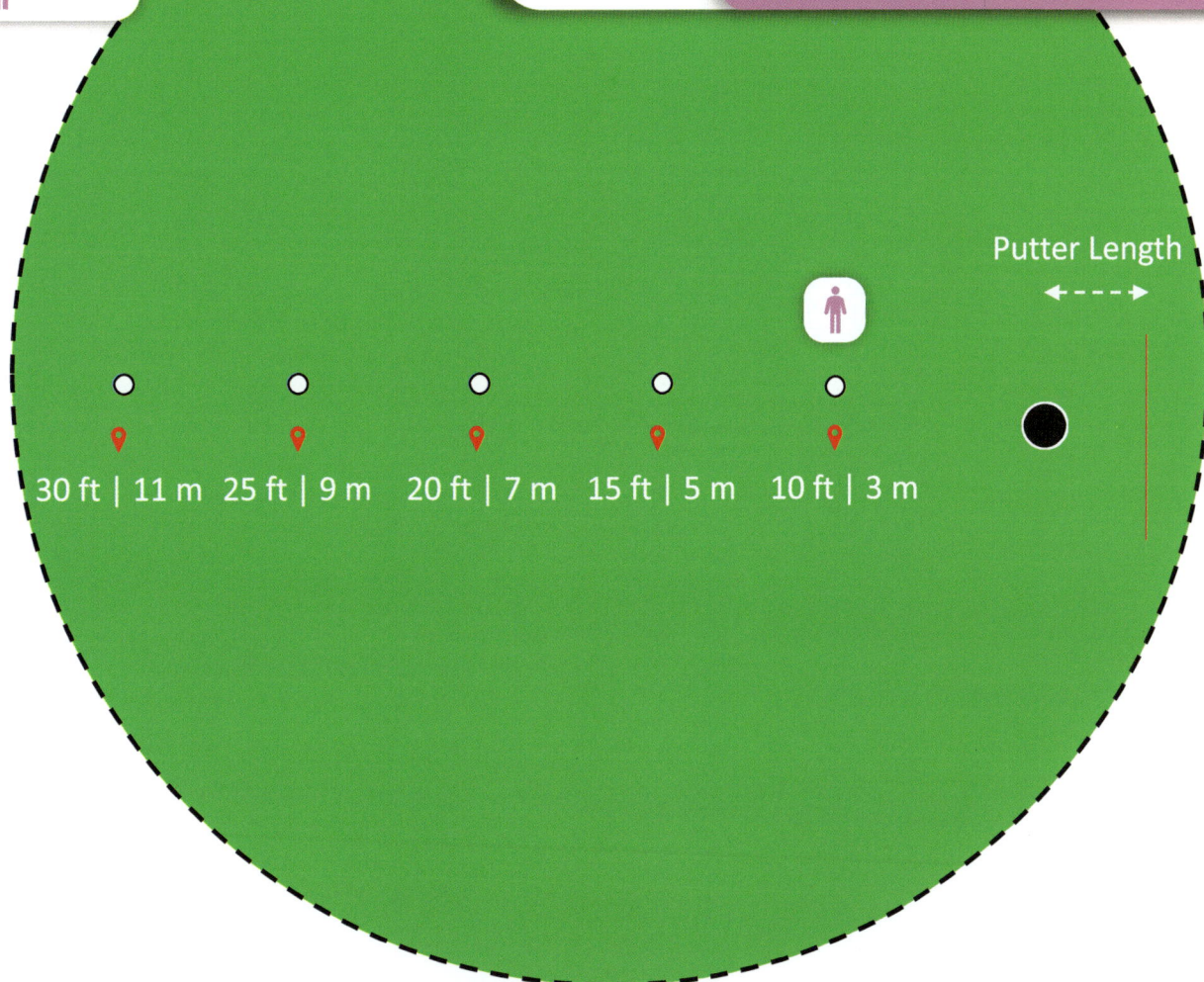

Putter Length

30 ft | 11 m   25 ft | 9 m   20 ft | 7 m   15 ft | 5 m   10 ft | 3 m

1033

Stop the Ball: to the Stick, Five Tees, in a Row

Stop five balls in a row between the hole and an alignment stick to complete the challenge. If miss, fall back two tees.

✓ The goal is to stop five successful putts in a row between the hole and an alignment stick; starting with the shortest putt from **[10 ft | 3 m[** and advancing to the longer putts. If at any time the ball stops outside the area, fall back two tees. Complete the challenge more than once.

Setup Position five tees at **[10,15,20,25,30 ft | 3,5,7,9,11 m]**. *Position an alignment stick behind the hole, at a distance of one and a half putter length.*

15 – 20 min

Designed for

- Technique
- Performance
- Aim/Alignment
- Precision/Accuracy
- Scoring

Primary Skills   *Secondary Skills*

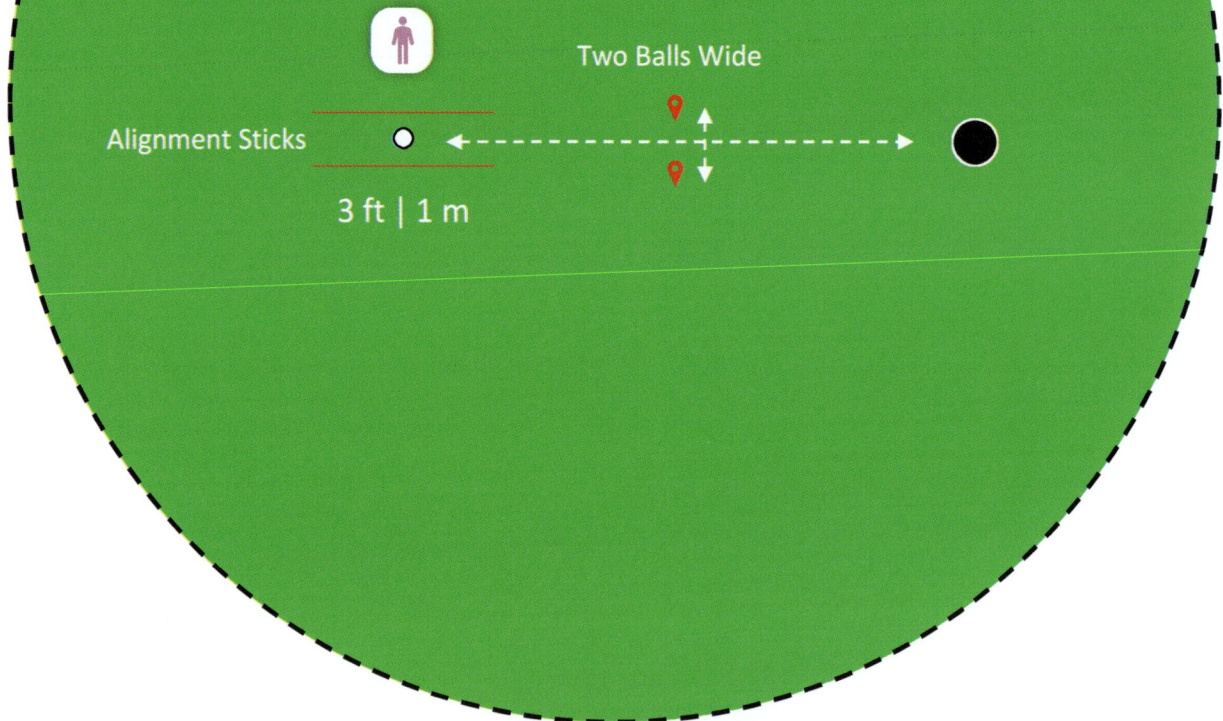

Two Balls Wide

Alignment Sticks

3 ft | 1 m

1038

Putting Aid: Alignment Sticks, Ball Gate, 50 in a Row

Make 50 putts in a row from in between two alignment sticks and through the ball gate.

✓ Make 50 putts in a row from **[3 ft | 1 m]**, in between the alignment sticks and through the ball gate.

Setup position two alignment sticks at *[3 ft | 1 m]*. The width between the sticks must be one putter head and two fingers. Ball gate must be half way to the hole and two balls wide.

Designed for

Primary Skills
- Technique
- Performance

Secondary Skills
- Aim/Alignment
- Precision/Accuracy
- Scoring

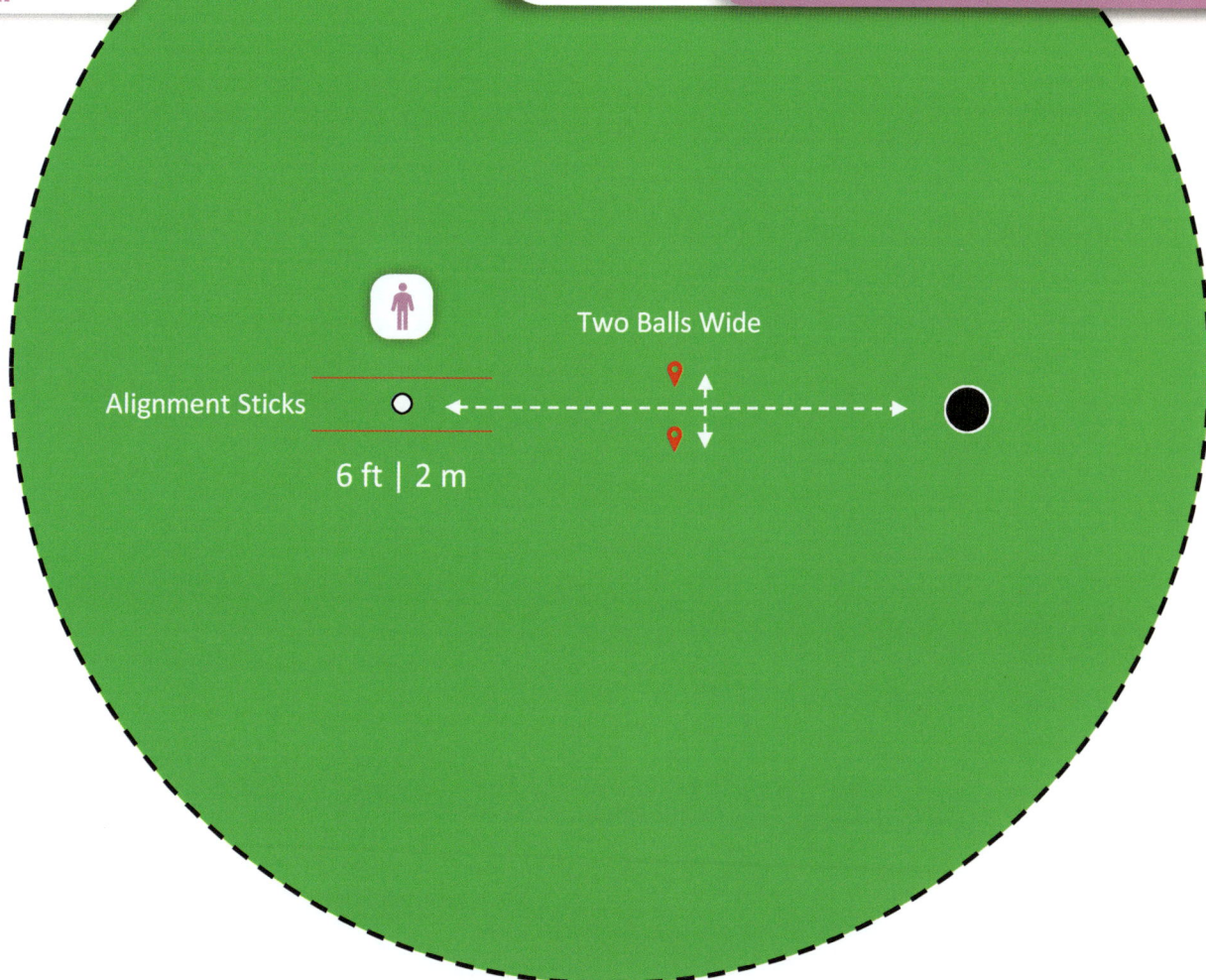

15 – 20 min

H

Two Balls Wide

Alignment Sticks

6 ft | 2 m

1039

Putting Aid: Alignment Sticks, Ball Gate, 15/25

Make 15 out of 25 putts from in between two alignment sticks and through the ball gate.

✓ To complete the challenge, must make 15 out of 25 putts from **[6 ft | 2 m]**, in between the alignment sticks and through the ball gate.

Setup position two alignment sticks at *[6 ft | 2 m]*. The width between the sticks must be one putter head and two fingers. Ball gate must be half way to the hole and two balls wide.

Designed for

Primary Skills
- Technique
- Performance

Secondary Skills
- Aim/Alignment
- Precision/Accuracy
- Scoring

15 – 20 min

H

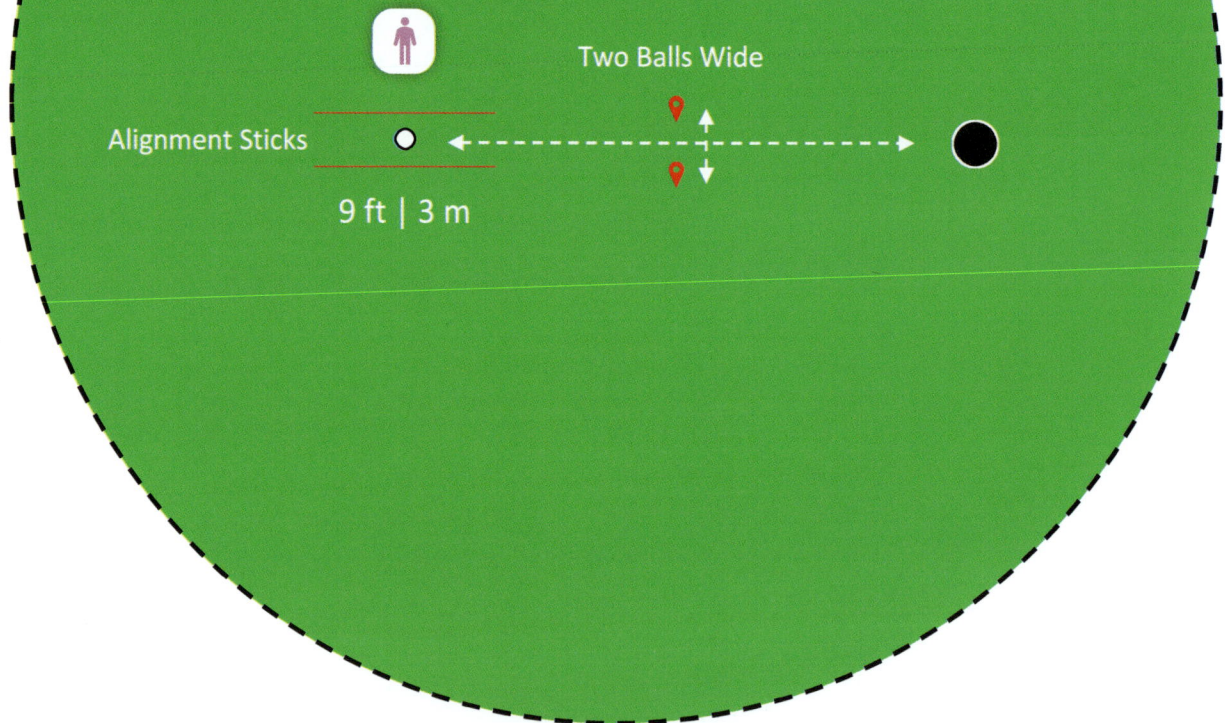

Two Balls Wide

Alignment Sticks

9 ft | 3 m

1040

Putting Aid: Alignment Sticks, Ball Gate, 10/20

Make 10 out of 20 putts from in between two alignment sticks and through the ball gate.

✓ To complete the challenge, must make 10 out of 20 putts from **[9 ft | 3 m]**, in between the alignment sticks and through the ball gate.

Setup* position two alignment sticks at [9 ft | 3 m]. The width between the sticks must be one putter head and two fingers. Ball gate must be half way to the hole and two balls wide.

M

15 – 20
min

Designed for

- Shot Shaping
- Precision/Accuracy
- Distance Control
- Visualization/Read

Primary Skills   *Secondary Skills*

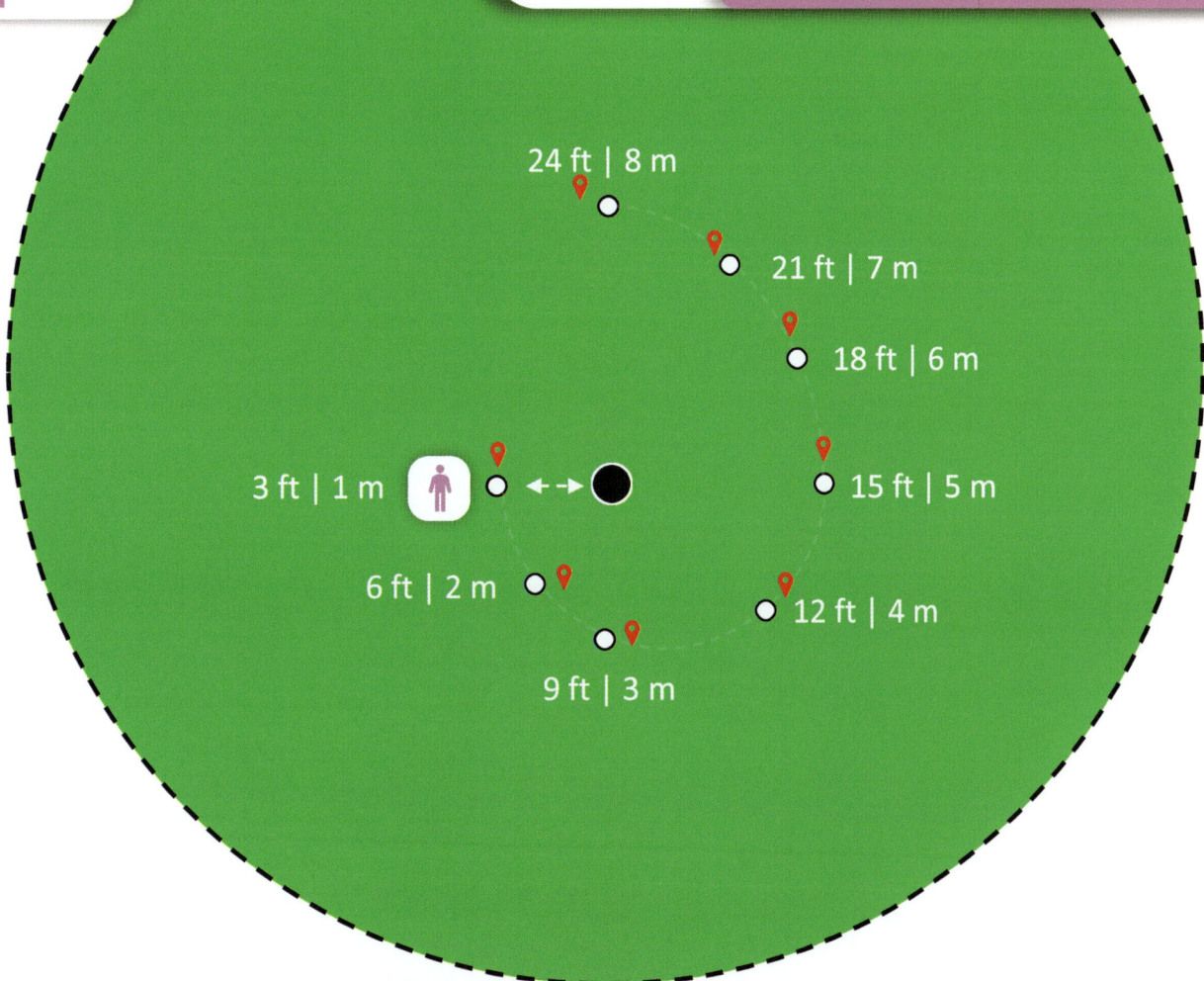

24 ft | 8 m

21 ft | 7 m

18 ft | 6 m

3 ft | 1 m

15 ft | 5 m

6 ft | 2 m

12 ft | 4 m

9 ft | 3 m

1059

Around the Hole: 8 Ball Spiral

Choose one of the approaches. Hit 40 balls.

✓ **Approach #1 – 5 balls per tee.** Start with the shortest putt. Hit 5 balls from a tee, then move to the next closest tee and hit 5 balls. Keep moving up the spiral until the last tee (hit 40 putts in total).

✓ **Approach #2 – 2 balls per tee.** Start with the shortest putt. Hit 2 balls from a tee, then move to the next closest tee and hit 2 balls. Keep moving up the spiral until the last tee (16 putts). Repeat the spiral two more times (48 putts in total).

✓ **Approach #3 – 2 balls per tee, randomly.** Hit 2 balls from a tee, then randomly jump to any other tee. Change tees at least 20 times (40 putts in total).

Setup* position 8 tees in [3 ft | 1 m] intervals, starting at [3 ft | 1 m]

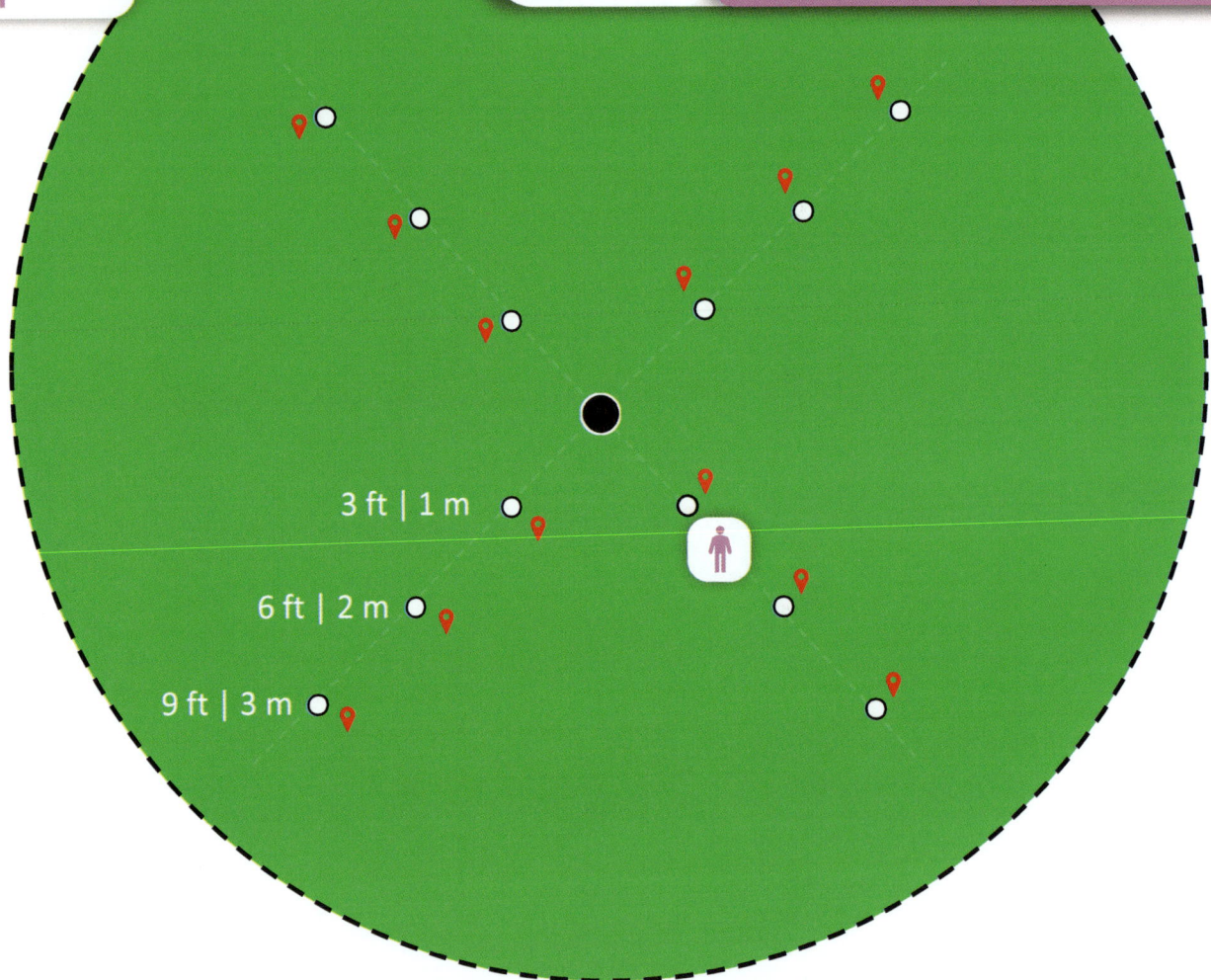

E ○ ○

15 – 20 min

Designed for

- Technique
- Shot Shaping
- Aim/Alignment
- Precision/Accuracy
- Distance Control
- Visualization/Read

Primary Skills | *Secondary Skills*

3 ft | 1 m

6 ft | 2 m

9 ft | 3 m

1060

Around the Hole: X Drill [Short]

Choose one of the approaches. Hit 36 balls.

✓ **Approach #1 – 3 balls per tee**. Start with the shortest putt at one side of the hole. Hit 3 balls from **[3 ft | 1 m]** then another 3 from **[6 ft | 2 m]** and another 3 from **[9 ft | 3 m]**. Once 9 balls are hit from one side of the hole, move to the next side of the hole and repeat. Progress through all four sides of the hole (hit 36 putts in total).

✓ **Approach #2 – 1 ball per tee**. Same setup as Approach #1. Hit 1 ball per tee and progress through all four sides of the hole three times in total (36 putts in total).

✓ **Approach #3 – 1 ball per tee, randomly**. Hit 1 ball from any given tee then randomly jump to any other tee. Make at least 40 jumps (40 putts in total).

*Setup** position three tees at four sides of the hole (12 tees in total)*

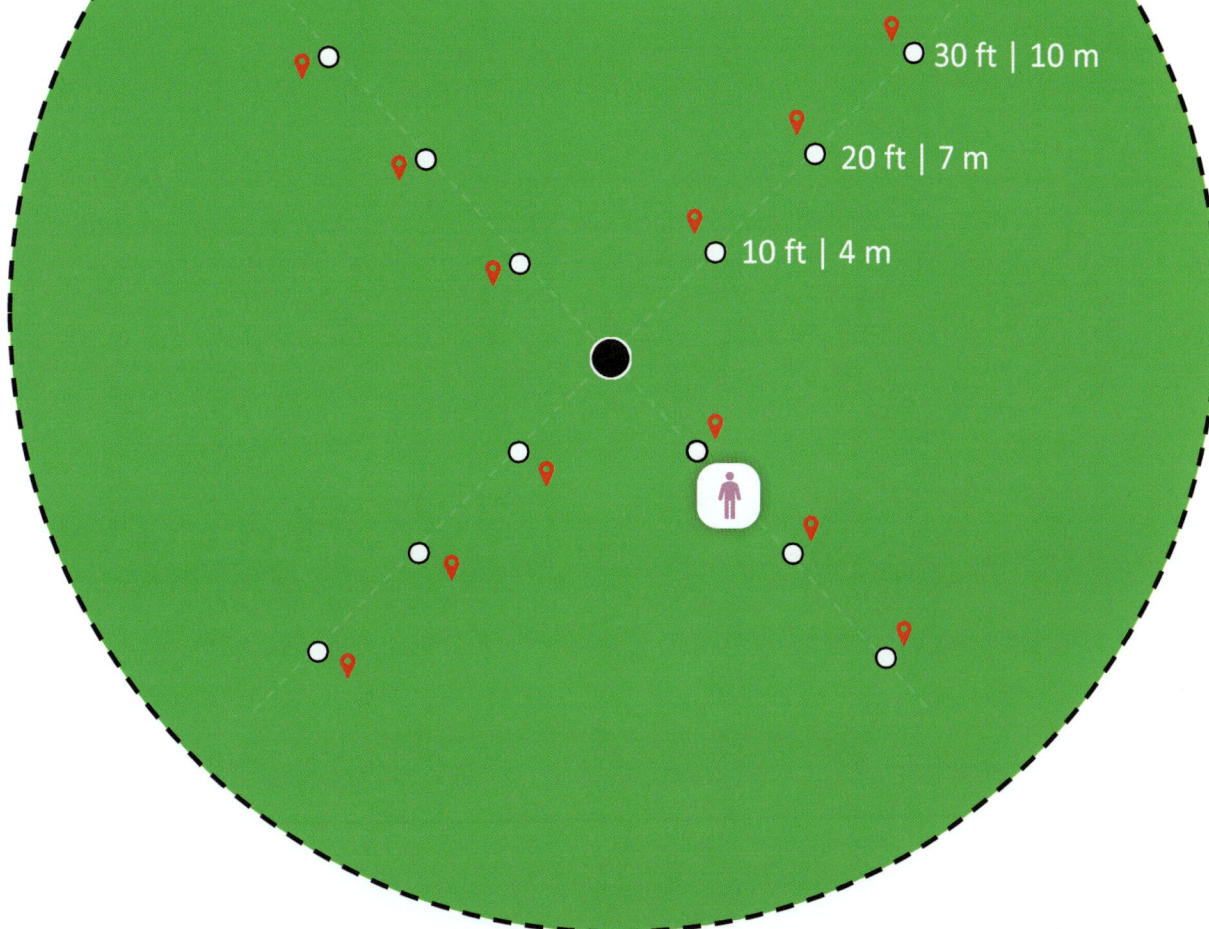

Short | Mid | Long

E ○ ○

15 – 20 min

Designed for

Primary Skills
- Technique
- Shot Shaping

Secondary Skills
- Aim/Alignment
- Precision/Accuracy
- Distance Control
- Visualization/Read

30 ft | 10 m
20 ft | 7 m
10 ft | 4 m

1062

Around the Hole: X Drill [Long]

Choose one of the approaches. Hit 36 balls.

✓ **Approach #1 – 3 balls per tee**. Start with the shortest putt at one side of the hole. Hit 3 balls from **[10 ft | 4 m]** then another 3 from **[20 ft | 7 m]** and another 3 from **[30 ft | 10 m]**. Once 9 balls are hit from one side of the hole, move to the next side of the hole and repeat. Progress through all four sides of the hole (hit 36 putts in total).

✓ **Approach #2 – 1 ball per tee**. Same setup as Approach #1. Hit 1 ball per tee and progress through all four sides of the hole three times in total (36 putts in total).

✓ **Approach #3 – 1 ball per tee, randomly**. Hit 1 ball from any given tee then randomly jump to any other tee. Make at least 40 jumps (40 putts in total).

Setup position three tees at four sides of the hole (12 tees in total)

E ◯ ◯

15 – 20 min

Designed for

- Shot Shaping
- Precision/Accuracy
- Visualization/Read

Primary Skills | *Secondary Skills*

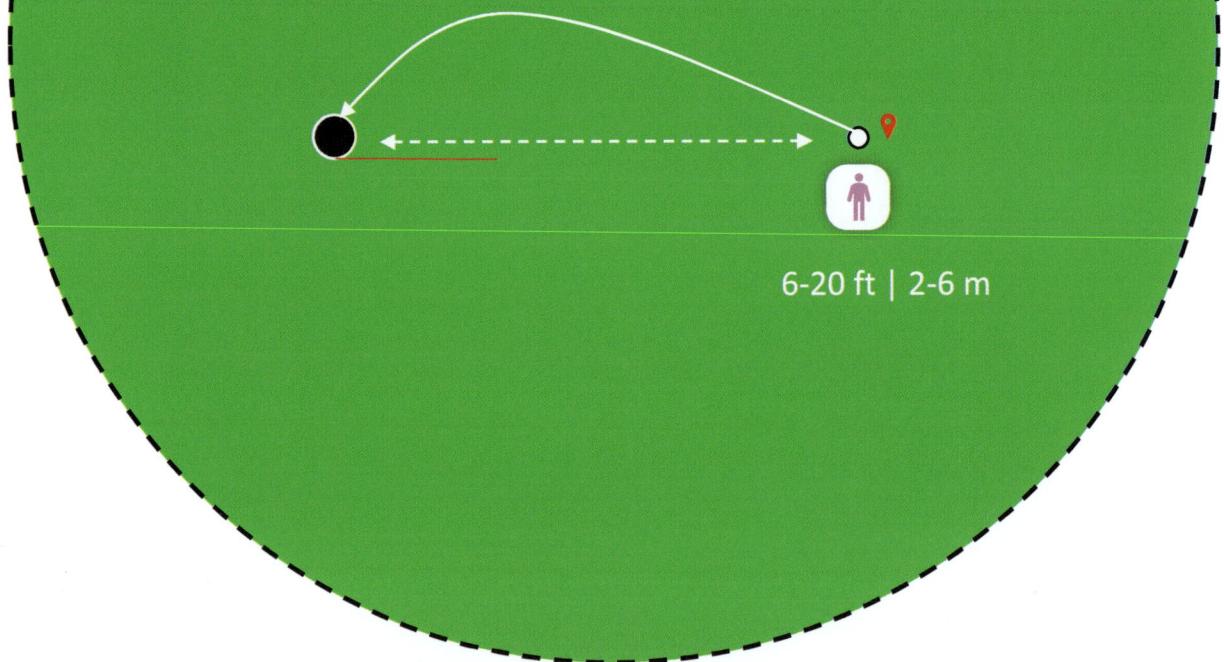

6-20 ft | 2-6 m

1068

High Side, Above the Stick

Hit 30 sloped putts without touching the alignment stick.

✓ The goal is to hole the putt on the high side of the hole, above the alignment stick, and without touching it. Hit 30 balls. Re-setup at a different distance and hit another 30 balls.

Setup* *Position a tee at [6,9,12,15 or 20 ft | 2,3,4,5 or 6 m]. Find a slope. Position an alignment stick such that it touches the bottom edge of the hole.*

M

15 – 20 min

Designed for

- Shot Shaping
- Precision/Accuracy
- Visualization/Read

Primary Skills   *Secondary Skills*

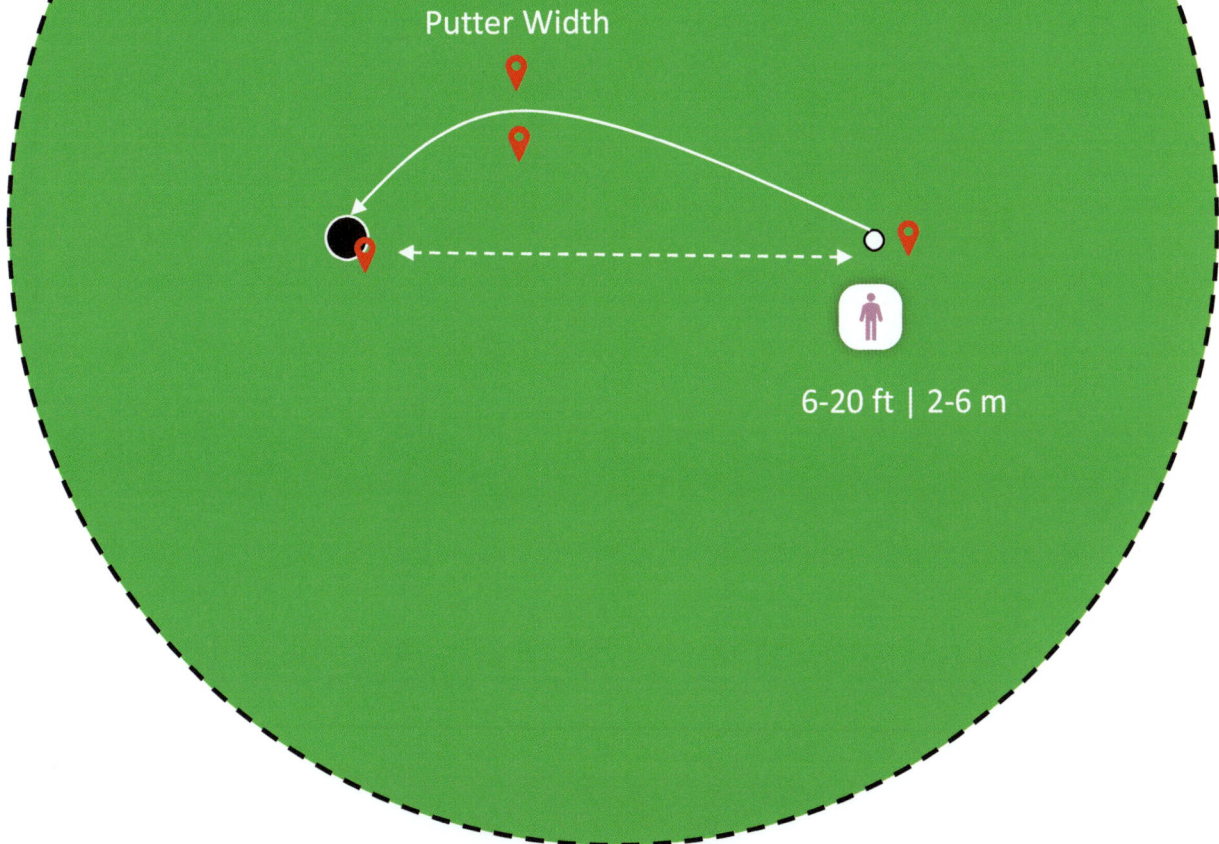

Putter Width

6-20 ft | 2-6 m

1069

High Side, Ball Gate – Peak of the Break

Hit 30 sloped putts above the tee (at the hole) and through the ball gate (high side of the putt).

✓ Position a tee at a given distance. Position two tees (putter width) at the peak of the break such that the ball passes through the ball gate. Position a tee at the bottom edge of the hole such that the ball passes above the tee. Hit 30 balls. Re-setup at another distance and hit another 30 balls.

Setup* Position a tee at [6,9,12,15 or 20 ft | 2,3,4,5 or 6 m].

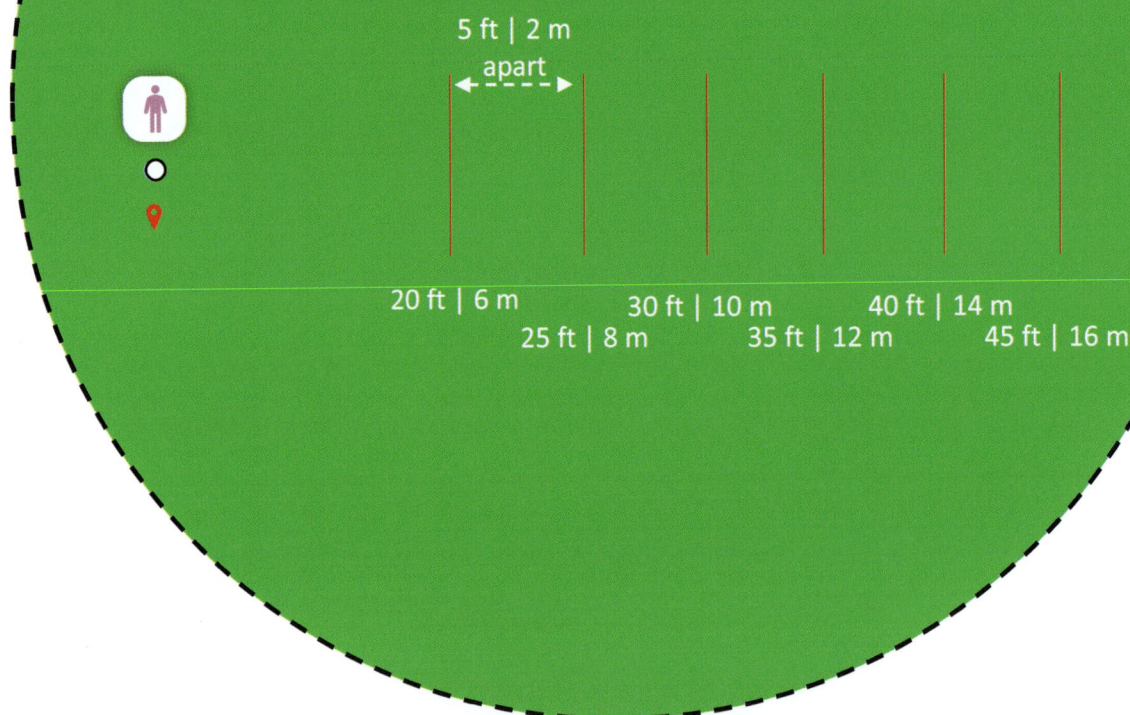

M

15 – 20 min

Designed for

- Shot Shaping
- Distance Control
- Visualization/Read

Primary Skills   *Secondary Skills*

5 ft | 2 m apart

20 ft | 6 m   30 ft | 10 m   40 ft | 14 m
     25 ft | 8 m   35 ft | 12 m   45 ft | 16 m

1071

Stop the Ball: Inside the Field [Long]

Stop the ball inside five fields to complete the challenge.

✓ **Approach #1 – short to long.** Start with the first field. Putt to the first (shortest) field until the ball stops inside the field. Once the ball stops inside the first field, advance to the next field. Putt until at least one ball has successfully stopped inside each of the five fields.

✓ **Approach #2 – randomly.** Start with any field. Putt to the selected field until the ball stops inside the field. Then randomly putt to any other field until at least one ball has stopped inside each of the five fields.

✓ Repeat the challenge more than once.

Setup* use 6 strings (or 12 tees) to make five fields [5 ft| 2 m apart] at [20,25,30,35,40,45 ft | 6,8,10,12,14,16 m]

H

15 – 20 min

Designed for

- Technique
- Aim/Alignment
- Precision/Accuracy
- Visualization/Read

Primary Skills *Secondary Skills*

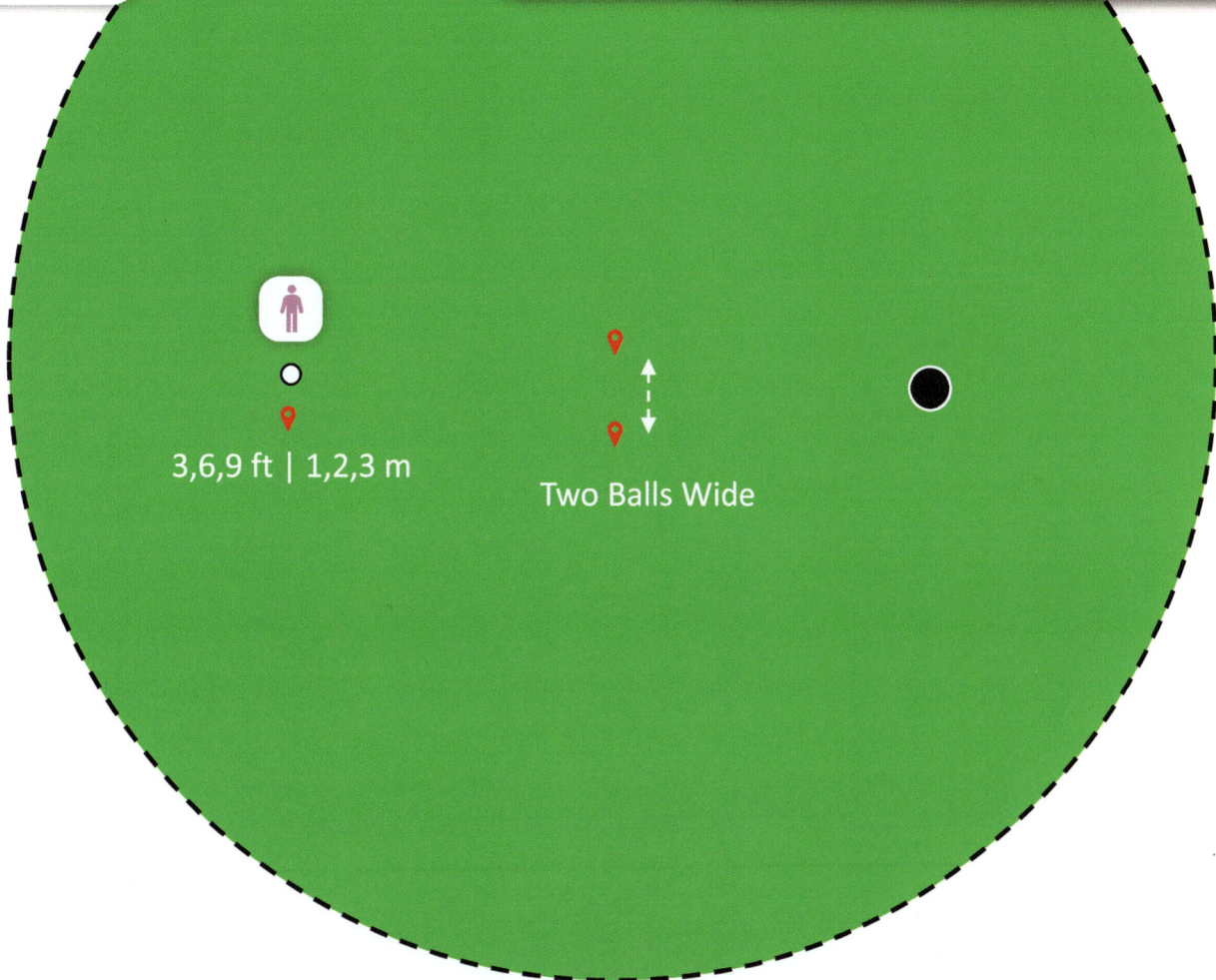

3,6,9 ft | 1,2,3 m

Two Balls Wide

1073

One Handed, Ball Gate

Hit 30 balls through the ball gate, one-handed.

✓ Hit 30 balls one-handed through the ball gate from **[3 ft | 1 m]**. Repeat the challenge more than once. Switch hands.

✓ Once finished with one distance, reposition tees to **[6 ft | 2 m]** and hit another 30 balls. Do the same for **[9 ft | 3 m]**.

Setup *position a tee at* **[3 ft | 1 m]** *and make a ball gate half way to the hole - position two tees (two balls wide).*

E ○ ○

15 – 20 min

Designed for

- Technique
- Shot Shaping
- Aim/Alignment
- Precision/Accuracy
- Distance Control

Primary Skills   *Secondary Skills*

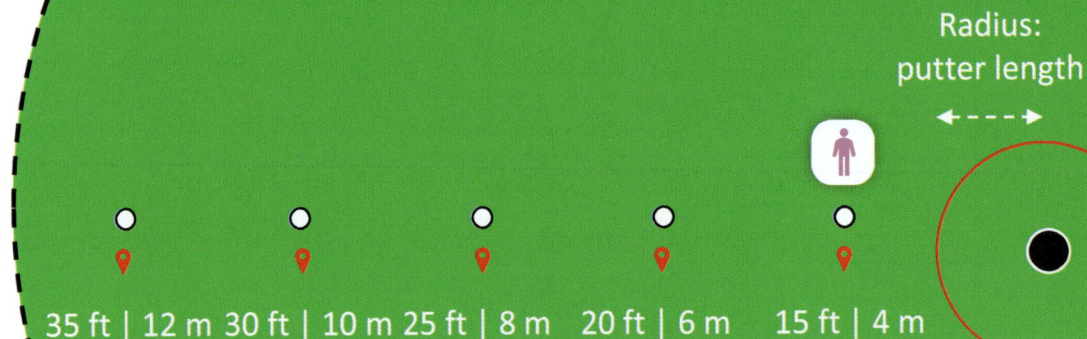

Radius:
putter length

35 ft | 12 m   30 ft | 10 m   25 ft | 8 m   20 ft | 6 m   15 ft | 4 m

1079

Stop the Ball: Circle, Five Tees [Mid - Long]

Stop the ball inside the circle from five tees.

✓ **Approach #1 – 10 balls per tee.** Hit 10 balls starting from the shortest tee at **[15 ft | 4 m]**. Then advance to the next tee and hit 10 balls and so until the last tee. Hit 50 putts in total.

✓ **Approach #2 – 10 balls per tee.** Same setup as Approach #1. Hit 10 balls starting from the furthest tee at **[35 ft | 12 m]**. Then advance to the next shorter putt. Hit 50 putts in total.

✓ **Approach #3 – 2 balls per tee, randomly.** Hit 2 balls starting from any tee. Then randomly jump to any other tee and again hit 2 balls. Make at least 25 jumps (50 putts in total).

Setup Position five tees at [15,20,25,30,35 ft | 4,6,8,10,12 m]. Use a string line to form a circle (radius is one putter length); or use several tees; or draw using chalk.*

E ◯ ◯

15 – 20 min

Designed for
- Shot Shaping
- Distance Control
- Visualization/Read

Primary Skills   *Secondary Skills*

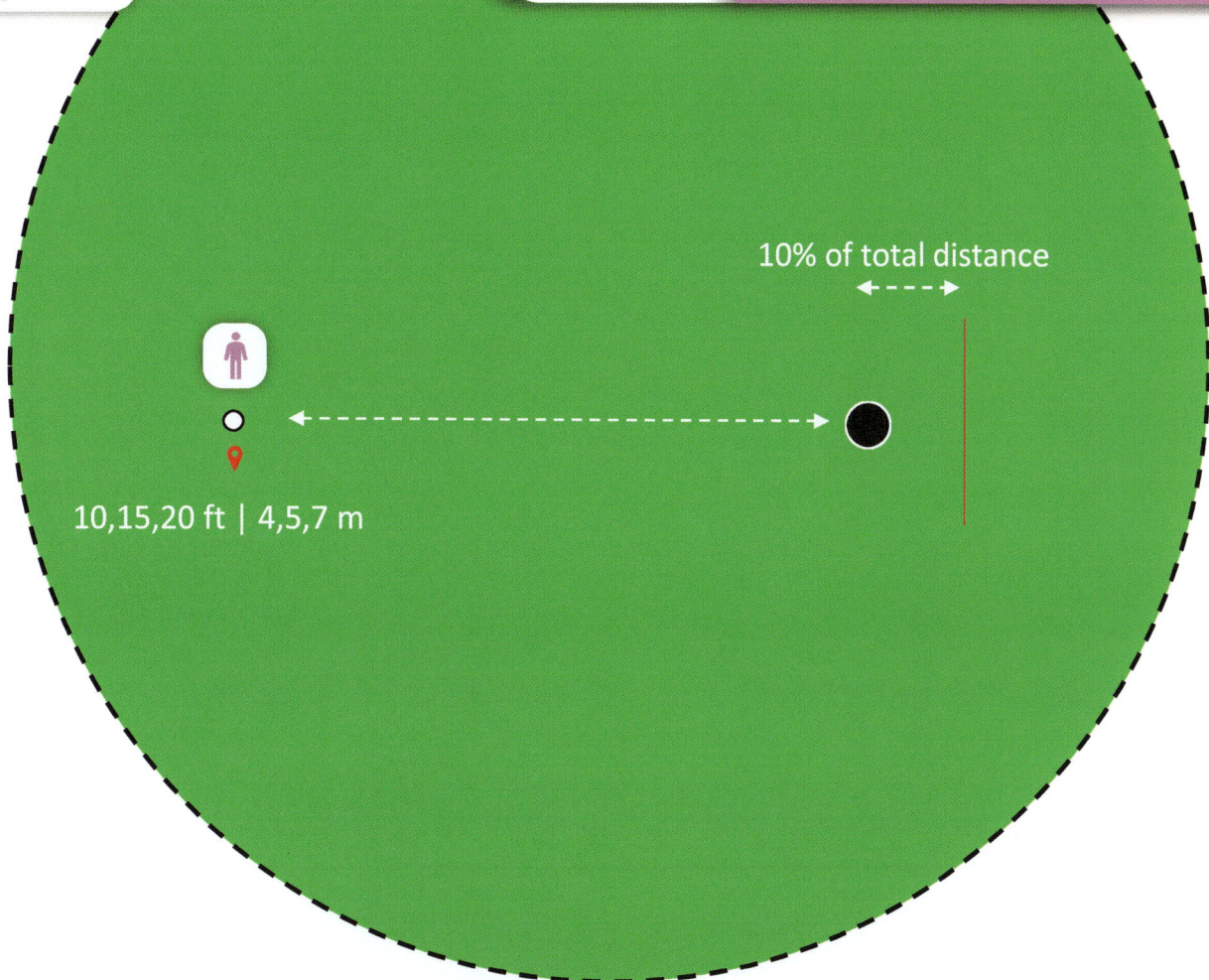

10% of total distance

10,15,20 ft | 4,5,7 m

1088

Stop the Ball: to the Stick [Mid]

Stop the ball past the hole and short of an alignment stick.

✓ Goal is to stop the ball past the hole and short of an alignment stick. Hit 30 balls from **[10 ft | 4 m]**. After 30 balls, reposition at **[15 ft | 5 m]** and hit another 30 balls. Then 30 balls from **[20 ft | 7 m]**.

Setup* *position a tee at a given distance as a starting point. Position an alignment stick at 10% of the total distance. If putt is **[15 ft | 5 m]** long, alignment stick is at **[1.5 ft | 0.5 m]**.*

Designed for
- Shot Shaping
- Distance Control
- Visualization/Read

E ◯ ◯

15 – 20 min

Primary Skills   *Secondary Skills*

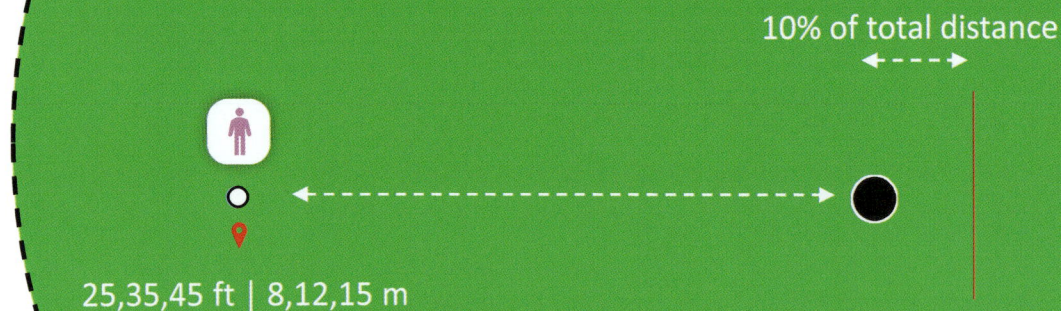

10% of total distance

25,35,45 ft | 8,12,15 m

1089

Stop the Ball: to the Stick [Long]

Stop the ball past the hole and short of an alignment stick.

✓ Goal is to stop the ball past the hole and short of an alignment stick. Hit 20 balls from **[25 ft | 8 m]**. After 20 balls, reposition at **[35 ft | 12 m]** and hit another 20 balls. Then 20 balls from **[45 ft | 15 m]**.

Setup* position a tee at a given distance as a starting point. Position an alignment stick at 10% of the total distance. If putt is [25 ft | 8 m] long, alignment stick is at [2.5 ft | 0.8 m].

E ○ ○

15 – 20 min

Designed for

- Technique
- Shot Shaping

- Aim/Alignment
- Distance Control
- Visualization/Read

Primary Skills   *Secondary Skills*

Two Feet

21 ft | 7 m   18 ft | 6 m   15 ft | 5 m   12 ft | 4 m   9 ft | 3 m

1092

Stop the Ball: to the Stick, Five Tees [Mid]

Stop the ball between the hole and an alignment stick from five tees.

✓ **Approach #1 – 10 balls per tee**. Hit 10 balls starting from **[9 ft | 3 m]**. Then advance to the next distance and hit 10 balls and so until the last tee. Hit 50 putts in total.

✓ **Approach #2 – 10 balls per tee**. Same setup as Approach #1. Hit 10 balls starting from **[21 ft | 7 m]**. Then advance to the next shorter tee and hit 10 balls. Hit 50 putts in total.

✓ **Approach #3 – 2 balls per tee, randomly**. Hit 2 balls starting from any tee. Then randomly jump to any other tee and again hit 2 balls. Make at least 25 jumps (50 putts in total).

Setup* Position five tees at [9,12,15,18,21 ft | 3,4,5,6,7 m]. Position an alignment stick behind the hole, at a distance of two feet.

E ○ ○

15 – 20 min

Designed for

- Shot Shaping
- Precision/Accuracy
- Visualization/Read

Primary Skills | *Secondary Skills*

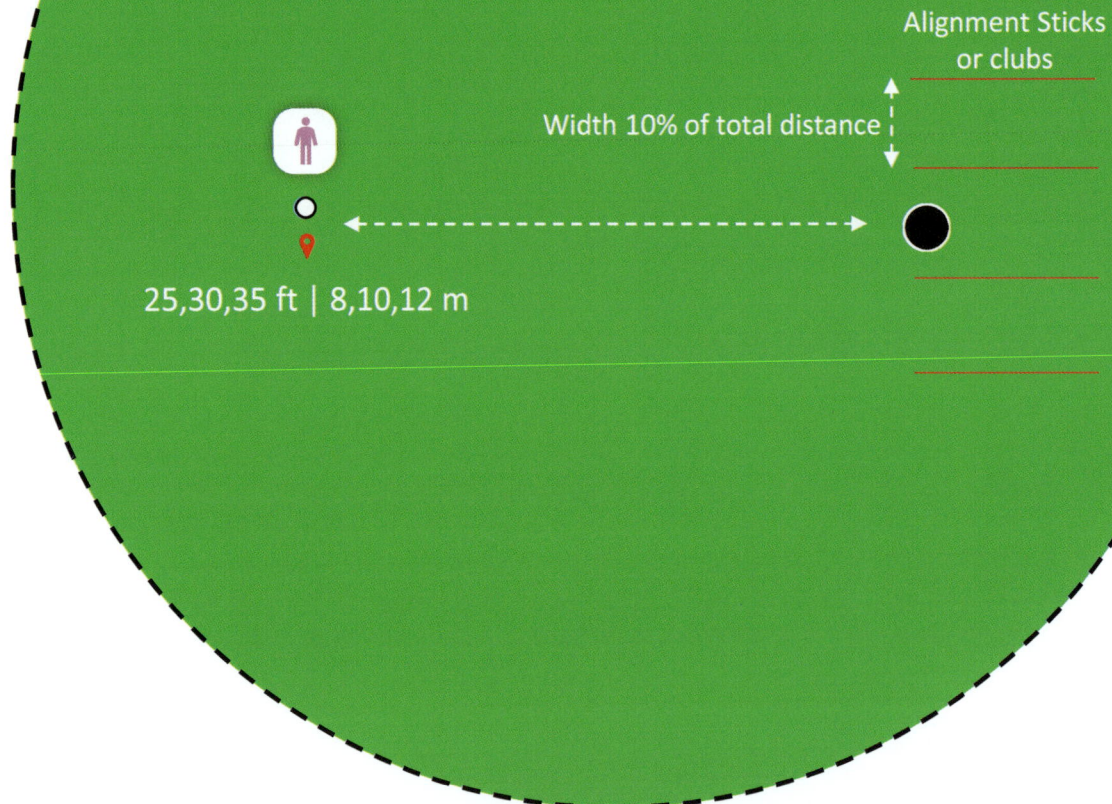

Alignment Sticks or clubs

Width 10% of total distance

25,30,35 ft | 8,10,12 m

1105

Three Gates Dispersion [Long]

Hit 30 balls and count how many balls end at which gate (to test for dispersion).

✓ Hit 30 balls from **[25 ft | 8 m]** and count how many balls end inside of each gate. After hitting 30 balls, reposition at **[30 ft | 10 m]** and hit another 30 balls. Then reposition at **[35 ft | 12 m]** and hit another 30 balls.

Setup* position a starting tee at [25,30 and/or 35 ft | 8,10 and/or 12 m]. Position four alignment sticks (or golf clubs) behind the hole. Width between the gates must be 10% of the total distance (i.e. [30 ft | 10 m] putt has gates at width of [3 ft | 1 m])

E ○ ○

15 – 20 min

Designed for

- Technique
- Shot Shaping
- Aim/Alignment
- Precision/Accuracy
- Visualization/Read

Primary Skills   *Secondary Skills*

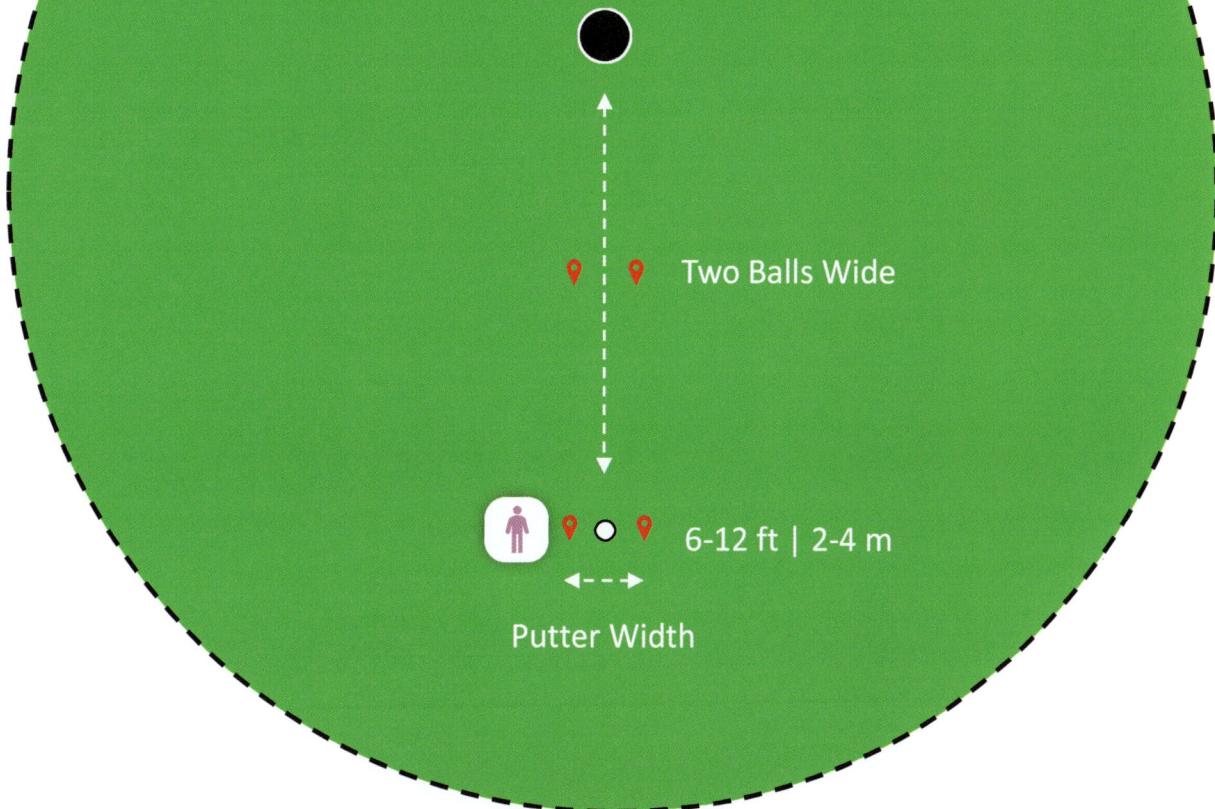

Two Balls Wide

6-12 ft | 2-4 m

Putter Width

1107

Through the Putter Gate and Ball Gate

Hit 30 balls through the ball gate such that the putter moves through the putter gate.

✓ Hit 30 balls through the ball gate from **[6 ft | 2 m]** such that the putter moves through the putter gate. After hitting 30 balls, reposition at **[9 ft | 3 m]** and hit another 30 balls. Then reposition at **[12 ft | 4 m]** and hit another 30 balls.

Setup *for a putter gate - position two tees at the width of one putter and one finger on each side. For a ball gate, position two tees half-way to the hole at the width of two balls.*

Keep Learning

Unlock more with subscription.

Subscribe to drills.golf and unlock

- ✓ **Full Access to the Online Library of Nearly 1,000 Drills**
- ✓ **Save Unlimited Drills to Favorites**
- ✓ Enter Scores and Get Practice Handicap
- ✓ **Download 700+ PDF Files** (*Download and Print Rights*)
- ✓ Export Entire Practice Programs in a PDF
- ✓ **Share Drills** via WhatsApp, Email and Social Media
- ✓ Get New Drill Alerts
- ✓ Add and Schedule Drills to Calendar

- ✓ **Create Practice Plans/Calendars**
- ✓ Send Custom Schedules
- ✓ Organize Drills into Folders
- ✓ **Create a Team**
- ✓ Invite Team Members
- ✓ Track Your Practice via Practice Log
- ✓ **Stay Informed with Analytics**
- ✓ Choose from 50+ Drill Templates

...and more

DRILLS.GOLF

[Subscribe Today]

Similar Drills

...that share the same characteristics as the drills in this eBook.

Putting **27 Drills**

Develop Competitive Mindset Drills

Gain confidence in your putting mechanics in preparation for a serious match. Develop competitive mindset using drills with tees, alignment sticks, putting mirror, strings, and other accessories. Learn how to control distance and hit the putt on the line.

Explore Collection

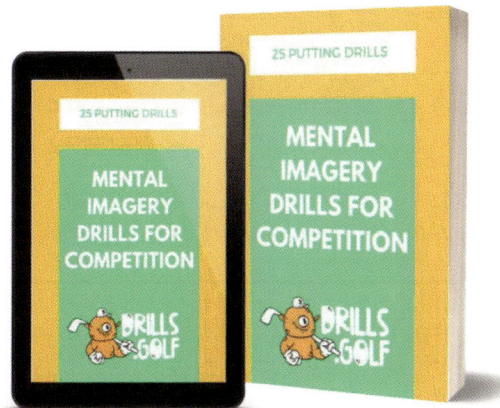

Putting **28 Drills**

Relaxing Drills for Mechanics

Get your putting mechanics in check using tees, alignment sticks, plane board, strings, and other aids. Learn technique with stress-free task-oriented drills – meaning that your only goal is to hit 40 putts in total, and not worry about holing any number of putts.

Explore Collection

Putting **25 Drills**

Mental Imagery Drills for Competition

Learn how to rely on mental imagery on the putting green using competitive drills without tees, alignment sticks and other aids. Develop trust in your swing as you learn how to score before the upcoming match.

Explore Collection

Driving Range **30 Drills**

Multi Purpose All-in-one Drills

Hand-picked drills from all other products packed in one single product. Discover strengths and weaknesses, improve wedge game, eliminate misses, progress through exercises, develop mental imagery skills – be it before a serious match or for fun.

Explore Collection

About the Author

Luka Karaula

From Portugal to United States, Mayakoba to PGA National, and Scotland to Philippines, I played more than 300 competitive rounds of golf in two decades, traced 90% of the low scores directly to golf practice and realized what works for me also works for others.

The real place where golf scores happen is before the round of golf, before the competition, when no one is watching. The hours you spend preparing and practicing, directly impact your scores, and the better your practice habits, the better your scores.

Golf takes time, no trophy is won over night. My purpose with drills.golf is to allow golfers to **spend 5 minutes to plan next 5 days of practice** – and to do it repeatedly. It took me more than 10.000 hours of practice, and roughly 1 million golf balls hit, to come to this simple truth – **make a plan, then make it happen**. There is a gradual system behind drills.golf, and each time you return is like building another block, same as building a pyramid, block by block.

Now that you have this ebook, you have the building blocks. You have the drills. I invite you to visit **drills.golf** where you can access a library of nearly 1,000 drills and learn how to build a pyramid of your own golf game, win your next match – or simply relax and learn. – Luka

Credentials 📜 🖊️

- *BA in Economics [**Seattle University, cum laude,** 2015]*
- Lifetime Honorary Member [**Omicron Delta Epsilon Society of Economists**, 2015]
- Sports Director [**Golf Club BJ**, 2015 - 2017]
- Team Advisor [**Croatian National Junior Golf Team**, 2016]
- CEO [2017], Supervisory Board Member
- [2018 - 2022] [**Croatian Golf Association**]
- Financial Advisory [**Deloitte TTL**, 2018]
- Professional Golfer [2020 - 2024]
- E-Commerce Business Owner [2020 - 2023]
- Club Fitter [**McGuirks Ireland**, 2024]
- Founder [**drills.golf**, 2024 – today]

Achievements ⛳ 🏆

- Scottish Boys Open, North Berwick Golf Club [**Won – 1st Place**, 2007]
- Croatian National Junior Golf Championship [**Won – 1st Place**, 2007 & 2010]
- Croatian Amateur Match Play Championship [**Won – 1st Place**, 2016]
- Croatian Amateur Championship [**Runner Up – 2nd Place,** 2010, 2015, 2016]
- Croatian Amateur Order of Merit [**Won – 1st Place**, 2010, 2015, 2016, 2017]
- Great American Conference Championship [**Won – 1st Place Team**, (NCAA DII) 2012]
- **All-Conference Squad/Honorable**

Mention [by Great American Conference (DII), 2012]
- **U.S. Amateur Qualifiers** [Washington State, US – Appearance 2014]
- **Men's Golf – Team Captain** – NCAA DI [Seattle University Golf Team, 2014/2015]
- **World Amateur Team Championship** [Mexico, Cancun – Appearance, 2016]
- **European Team Shields Championship** [Appearances in 2015, 2016, 2017]
- Croatian PGA Championship [**Runner Up – 2nd Place**, 2021]

Printed in Great Britain
by Amazon